OBJECTIVE LOVE

I0140052

Megan Terry
directed and
structured by
Jo Ann Schmidman

BROADWAY PLAY PUBLISHING INC
224 E 62nd St, NY, NY 10065
www.broadwayplaypub.com
info@broadwayplaypub.com

First printing: November 2012
I S B N: 978-0-88145-539-7
Book design: Marie Donovan
Typographic controls & page make-up: Adobe InDesign
Typeface: Palatino
Printed and bound in the U S A

CHARACTERS & SETTING

HE
SHE
ACTOR 1
ACTOR 2
ACTOR 3
ACTOR 4
ACTOR 5

Note: HE *and* SHE *are played by the same actors throughout the play.*

Because of the nature of the piece, the number of actors may be greater or fewer depending on how many actors are available.

Time: Present

DESIGN NOTES

The set may be designed, as we did in Omaha, with a small or no budget and lots of creative energies. At the Omaha Magic Theatre our basic environment was white and black. We stretched white opaque plastic over a 10' x 15' collapsible pipe frame to serve as a ground for the backdrop design. White plastic curtains cover two 3-1/2' openings far left and far right. The entire floor area was covered with white plastic. If you have the resources, it would be ideal to cover the entire theater space in white plastic. The audience may be asked to remove their shoes in the lobby area before entering. Perspective and vanishing point "visual goofs" drawn in black electrical tape on the white plastic are recurring motifs. Floor lines begin broad and vanish into the backdrop.

We made the clothes "new wave" by adding geometric designs and lines with black or white tape (electrical tape or that used for graphic layout borders). He and She costumes which have color, are displayed like paper doll clothing. These are backed by shirt cardboard with folded fabric or tissue paper at neck, sleeve, etc—in this way they are made to look flat (one-dimensional) and will always be worn as clothes displayed in a catalog (free of wrinkles and hanging perfectly). Clothes are put on like regular clothing when indicated in the script.

SPECIAL EQUIPMENT

Two slide projectors, two crankies which serve as teleprompters (or actual) teleprompters if they can be borrowed). The crankies sit on a platform built atop two 6 foot ladders. The slide projectors sit on platforms built out on the ladders where the paint tray usually rests. Caution must be taken to make ladder stationary.

Sound Jam: Each actor must intricately score the plant speech, perfecting and committing to memory each beat and intention change. The director should work with each actor separately for a long time before attempting the jam. When each actor is completely rehearsed and secure, put the two together. A jam will take place if the actors are true to their worked out rhythms and are "simply aware" of the other actors' words.

(*At curtain, lights are dimmed and slides of beautiful living things are projected on two areas of the backdrop—ten slides from each projector alternate and overlap. screen right: flowers and plants growing outside or in a greenhouse… screen left: animals—domestic, zoo or wild. [note: when slides are used elsewhere in the production, six slides from each projector alternate in a similar manner.]*)

(HE *and* SHE *move to their places.* HE *to right side of platform,* SHE *to left. Each assumes several different attitudes as they model their first outfit. They try on these attitudes as if they have been printed on their and faces.*)

(*Two actors enter through white curtains left and right. Each pulls a black hood over her head as they move downstage to the cubes; they mount the cubes.*)

ACTORS: I object. (*In unison. They remove hoods and exit.*)

(*Several* ACTORS *enter; they carry beautiful flowers—some are made of paper, some silk, some are carved from wood and dance on vibrating wires, others are delicate shell flowers; there are linen flowers and flowers that grow in a fish bowl, even ceramic flower chimes. Actors move around the set looking for a "perfect spot" to place these flowers. An individual actor may say: "eye object" if this placement/ design looks right.* ACTORS *may try several spots and question if it makes an: "eye object". They may stand back from their arrangement, look and respond objectively: "eye object". Some may admire the flowers and lovingly say "eye object".*)

(SHE *changes pose on her platform and sounds chimes.*)

(ACTORS 1 *and* 2 *assume the following characters and address the audience.*)

WOMAN: Hi, I'm ninety-four.

CHILD: I'm ten.

WOMAN: Hi, I don't know how many children I have.

CHILD: Hi, I don't know how much money I'm going to make.

(SHE *changes pose and sounds chimes. At the sound, all* ACTORS *respond as if a thought has just occurred to them. They move with their flowers to the perfect spot and place them. Three actors move to plastic flower pots downstage and plant their "flowers".*)

ONE *or* TWO ACTORS: Eye object.

(*Admiring*)

(SHE *sounds chimes. Two* ACTORS *upstage change their minds; they grab their plant object, move downstage to flower pots and begin to work. A sound jam ensues. [note: turn to appendix B for sound jam direction.*)

(ACTORS *with plants, potting soil, water can and empty pots enter and begin to work with the plants.*)

ACTORS 1 & 2: (*Speech to audience*) I'm going to plant this baby. My grandmother had a green thumb. Plants keep me alive. Human beings breathe plant exhaust. Plants breathe our exhaust. It's an efficient universe.

(*Each speaks directly, lovingly to plants as they pick up plants and pots*).

ACTORS 1 & 2: I love the furry feelings of your leaves. This color in your center is so compelling. I'd love to bite it. "Marigolds are brain food."

(*Both move through space with their newly potted plants. Other* ACTORS *enter with water in various forms—a big glass bowl, marbles in bottom, filled with water; a sponge*

absorbing and squeezing water into a square glass container;
a spray bottle filled with water; a glass of water and a straw.
These ACTORS *and the two* ACTORS *with potted plants*
slowly chase each other through the space. They continue
during the he and she lines.)

(HE *wears a "preppy" red sport coat and subtly striped*
pants. both hang on him as if he were a "paper doll." The
garments are glued to cardboard backing to give this "paper
doll" effect, the clothing will always look as if it would
never wrinkle—it always "hangs" perfect. SHE *wears a very*
sophisticated, hot pink dressing gown with baby blue sash.
HE *and* SHE *each stay on their own side of the platform and*
read their lines from the teleprompters as they pose to best
show off their clothes.)

HE: Take your hand away from your eye.

SHE: Idon't have my hand on my eye.

HE: Being exact isn't my thing.

SHE: When did I have my hand over my eye?

HE: I didn't say over, I said away. I don't want you to
create wrinkles around your eyes.

SHE: I don't want to create wrinkles around my eyes.
Do you think I look forward to wrinkles?

HE: That's why I'm cautioning you—you like to look at
you as much as I do.

SHE: I do like to check up on my looks.

HE: Please don't see my suggestions as criticism. If I
help you to overcome bad eye habits, then we can both
enjoy your skin as long as possible.

SHE: I rub aloe around my eyes and mouth everyday.

HE: Show me the direction.

SHE: I know what I'm doing. I do it everyday—
sometimes twice!

HE: You may be rubbing the wrong way—let me check you out.

SHE: I break off a thick frond and squash the end, then I rub it across my skin. Aloe erases wrinkles before they start.

HE: That's good, very good—it was your translucent skin that first attracted me to you…then I saw your eyes. I have a question… Wait…that's correct—the way you're rubbing your left side, but incorrect on your right eye.

SHE: Reverse directions on my right eye?

HE: Yes, around your eye. Do it that way. Rub in reverse. Not so hard. You're exerting too much force. Don't pressure your skin. You'll pull your skin too far away from the muscle. We don't want you sagging.

SHE: Not yet.

(ACTORS *come together down center, two actors form a chaise, others form elements of a "genteel flower garden and fountain setting" —young person [*ACTOR 4*] with spray bottle speaks and sprays. The* ACTOR *with the sponge washes her as she speaks;* ACTOR *with glass and straw offers her a drink, etc.*)

ACTOR 4: I love water. I know I'm only twenty-two, but water's been around for a billion years. (*She reclines on chaise.*) I figure I can learn a lot from water.

(*The washing rite is completed.*)

(HE *and* SHE *change costumes—he into a military jacket, she into a black gossamer, flowing, somewhat ominous gown.*)

(*Music: a door chime plays "God bless this home".* HE *grins broadly.* SHE *is worried.* SHE *climbs to the top of a pole up right.* HE *sits on platform edge up right.* SHE *reads from teleprompter right,* HE *is overly calm—a top executive looking very uncomfortable underneath his smile and relaxed position.)*

(Music: odd mechanical sounds come from moog or one of those battery operated ray guns with five different sounds [noted by "X"]. When sound occurs, the other ACTORS *transform into "hunted" or "hunter." [suggested intentions are: to torture; to idolize; to mask; to ignore; to attack…] after sound ends, actors make a barricade with their bodies, individually. Manikin parts are also used by the* ACTORS *to create barriers.)*

HE: *(X)* What I like about you, when you look like that, is the absence of cunning.

SHE: *(X)* It's an advancement in our generation… in our desire to be civilized.

HE: *(X)* Yes… the look of cunning—which mere thinking can produce on the face *(X)* does make one think of the animal *(X)*.

SHE: I know what you mean, the look of isolation.

(Musical cue: a stick is smacked percussively on floor. All actors except HE *and* SHE *dive to floor for safety.* HE *moves through obstacle course created by* ACTORS *and manikin parts. Music: constant beeping—throughout this section, lines are to be delivered rapidly.)*

HE: The look from the cave.

SHE: The look down the tree at the Grizzly.

HE: Live defensively.

SHE: The look of a survivor.

HE: A member of the food chain.

SHE: The look of the driver at rush hour.

HE: Looking for the shortest line at Safeway check-out.

SHE: Not the look we covet for ourself.

(All ACTORS *except* HE *and* SHE *line up in front of backdrop—backs to audience.* HE *lounges and poses according to his interior image of himself.)*

HE: Get rid of that word.

SHE: Which?

HE: Covet.

SHE: Right.

(Music: stick smacks on floor. The ACTORS, *now in a line, strike an isolation, heads up, reaching…they then move stage right or left and exit.)*

SHE: I get it.

HE: We have new choices.

(Other ACTORS *reenter holding empty picture frames over their faces—some squint wildly behind picture frames. The frames are held up either framing faces in profile or the face full front. Then an* ACTOR *may move to a manikin so that the framed image is that of that of the actor's face relating to a manikin's knee or perhaps a manikin's hand is thrust in a human mouth and framed for a momentary objective "look.")*

SHE: That survivor look does cause tiny teeny wrinkles right here in the corners under the eyes.

HE: My father had that look from reading the stock market page squinting for ups and downs.

SHE: My father had that look, squinting through his shot gun sight during duck hunting season.

HE: The squint of a winner.

SHE: Sweat beads his upper lip.

*(*ACTORS *continue to work with their picture frames.* SHE *slowly descends pole, still worried.* SHE *crosses to left side of platform.* HE *stands right side of platform. Both hold a chiffon veil over their faces. The veil is made tight by gluing*

it between two dowels. Slanted eye shapes are cut out for seeing.)

(HE and SHE work on eye isolations. They testify with only an expression, a movement, or rhythm changes of eye movements. Allow time for these images to occur.)

(SHE sounds chimes. Actors with picture frames move center—their faces framed, they squint. They try to figure out sound.)

(Black out. Colored abstract shapes from slide projector are projected onto these actors. The frames are collected as these ACTORS move stage left around stationary cube. they react to the light and color.)

(Lights up.)

(One ACTOR climbs on downstage left cube platform and places a black hood over his face and says, "I object" —black out.)

(Old family photographs are projected onto two areas of the white plastic backdrop in a definite rhythm of change and overlap.)

(HE and SHE dress. HE dons a white jacket and a blue hat; she, a pink leather cocktail dress.)

(An artist, with light in the eyes, sits on cube stage left. She looks at a favorite old photo, then clutches it to her breast. Slides of her photos appear near or above her.)

ACTOR 5: I love photographs taken before 1930. That, to me, is the true youth of America. Focusing backward, also, keeps me from getting hung up on my own image. When I meditate on a photo from a thrift shop or a garage sale, I can get to nirvana faster than when I chant transcendental mantras while gazing at a Hindu Mandala from the 15th century. That Mandala served me well until I discovered photos—antique photos. *(She places photograph on cube and stands so she can look at the photo from a distance.)* Concentrating on old photos helps me not to violate my deepest feelings for Americana and Eastman Kodakism. *(Intimately to audience, as she mounts cube.)* I no longer wish to tolerate interior schisms in the psychic sections of my brain. Love of pre-1930 shapshots makes my synapses hum and allows me to practice my religion imagistically and also to indulge my blatant nationalism.

(Three other ACTORS *enter, gather around base of cube and hold photos up to artist.)*

ACTOR 5: As a purist I don't use a magnifying glass, but I do sometimes have to soak my photos in apple cider vinegar to remove mildew or spider webs. I spend all my free time with my collection and view them one by one with my naked eye.

(Artist takes photos one at a time from the ACTORS—*she will treasure them.)*

(Black out: then more slides of old photgruphs. Mechanical beeping sounds—beep, beep, beep, beep. The ACTORS *walk in a circular path mechanically swaying their arms. They look very bored. They continue this action and follow one another through the first part of the scene.)*

*(*HE *and* SHE *stand together on left side of platform. They feel they clearly are better than those who sway their arms.* HE *and* SHE *pose, then change poses.* HE *reads from a teleprompter stage right.* SHE *from teleprompter stage left.)*

ACTOR 1: I love my job.

HE: They worry me as much as my father's generation used to.

ACTOR 1: I can't wait to get to work.

ACTOR 2: Me too.

SHE: We made a pact. Worry is out.

*(*ACTORS *1, 2 and 3 keep "zombie walking".)*

ACTOR 2: My filing cabinets are full of *Playboy* visions and "if it bleeds, it leads" realities.

ACTOR 3: I like my job too. We have Blue Cross, Blue Shield; the company pays into our retirement and I can build up to a whole four weeks vacation if I stay only fifteen years.

ACTOR 1: What a good deal!

ACTOR 3: It really is good.

HE: I can't help it. They're everywhere.

SHE: The younger people?

HE: Right.

(Rapid mechanical sound. ACTORS who have been walking zombie-like move to stage right cube. They sit, stand or kneel. Each selects one part of body to move. They are so bored it is amazing that a finger can be lifted or that a strand of hair can move. Whatever the selected movement, it is repeated—this is the one move that the actors can make.)

ACTOR 2: My dad got canned from Standard Oil two years before he was supposed to retire.

ACTOR 1: Wow, look at the pension they saved.

ACTOR 3: Why'd they do it?

ACTOR 2: He didn't do things by "the book." They said he was too "innovative."

ACTOR 3: You really get off on filing.

ACTOR 2: It's the best job yet. I don't have to think.

(They continue minimal moves as HE and SHE speak.)

SHE: I know what you mean. They have that look.

HE: They want jobs.

SHE: Dumb jobs.

HE: Work …

SHE: For other people.

HE: I can't imagine anyone wanting to work for anyone.

SHE: You should work for yourself.

HE: Absolutely.

(Rapid sound, a different one than before. actors begin doing a series of repeated movements: [1] lift shoulder; [2] bend elbows; [3] move arms back and forth four times; [4] drop arms and repeat. each actor does this series at own speed. it is not done in unison or like a machine exercise.)

ACTOR 2: I don't have to think

ACTOR 1: What a relief.

ACTOR 2: Nobody bothers me. I can fantasize all day long. I don't even have to talk except at coffee break.

ACTOR 1: What do you file?

ACTOR 2: Breasts, bottoms, hunks...

ACTOR 3: For the company?

ACTOR 2: Energy audits for O P P D. Little maps of homes from a bird's eye view. The houses glow around the places where energy is escaping into the cold...little glowing auras of sweet hot flesh

(Others join her).

ALL: Long sensuous thermal legs, moist heat mouths, insulated bedroom eyes, heat-pump hair, solarized tongues, double paneled hands, throbbing thermostats.

(Stop movements, sighing)

ALL: I love my job.

(Begin mechanical filing movements again).

SHE: We may be the first and last generation free to be. *you* and *me.*

HE: I hate to admit it.

(ACTORS *pick up soft-sculpture dice and have a crap-shoot downstage center.*)

(HE *and* SHE *change costumes. she wears a poodle skirt; a black rhinestoned cardigan sweater—it is stuffed with cardboard. she places it on her "paper doll" clothes.* HE *wears a beret, a hawaiian shirt and carries a flash camera.* HE *jumps off platform.*)

HE: Hold still.

(*The* ACTORS *freeze.* SHE *continues to pose.* HE *arranges the* ACTORS *as he would furniture in a room.* HE *places umbrellas in their hands to adjust for proper photographic light.* SHE, *after much time passes, notices that* HE *isn't looking at her. He is arranging them. both* HE *and* SHE *read from teleprompter left.*)

SHE: What is it?

HE: Don't look frantic, hold it.

(HE *begins to photograph* SHE *gymnastically.* HE *lies down, leans, shoots the photos from every imaginable position as if this is what makes a good photo.*)

SHE: Am I frowning?

HE: (*Focusing camera*) Don't think.

SHE: What are you after?

HE: Don't talk.

SHE: Did you see something?

HE: It was perfect before, let's try to get back to it.

SHE: I prefer your rayon Hawiian to the cotton.

HE: Don't. Comparisons—spoil your expression.

(SHE *is perfectly blank.*)

HE: That's it!! (*Clicks camera*)

(ACTORS *enter singing, "I object." all* ACTORS *except* HE *and* SHE *exit.*)

(Fashion parade begins—each ACTOR *enters and goes
through series of poses, wearing a favorite article of clothing.*
HE *puts on a cardboard backed gold lame jacket.* SHE *puts
on a satin jockey jacket. Both pose.* SHE *crosses to right side
of platform.* HE *lounges against platform.* SHE *begins to
rub* HE *all over.* SHE *reads from teleprompter left,* HE *from
right.* HE *is very cool. it is as though she is going through an
exercise in "come on" while he observes.)*

SHE: I like to think about you while I wait for you.

HE: Exterior or essence?

SHE: The smell of your sweatshirt.

HE: What else?

SHE: The shape of your eyelids.

HE: What else?

SHE: Your hot skin in summer.

HE: What else?

SHE: My hand gripping your thick hair.

HE: What else?

SHE: Walking toward me in cutoffs.

HE: What else?

SHE: *(She throws* HE *down.)* That's it.

*(*ACTORS *keep posing in favorite clothes.* HE *stays collapsed.
A vendor enters with soft-sculpture tomatoes, arranges other
*ACTORS *in fixed positions, then in poses with tomatoes, i.
e. covering breasts, in front of face, as a hat, as a bottom…
vendor takes a place and poses with tomatoes.)*

*(*HE *and* SHE *change costumes.* HE *wears a long blue
overcoat and top hat. she, a period, gold and blue, striped
gown hung on cardboard—which* SHE *wears like "paper
doll" clothes.)*

(At an open market)

ACTOR 5: I love these beefsteak tomatoes.

ACTOR 3: I object!

ACTOR 5: *(Continues to squeeze tomatoes)* I haven't ever—Ella Mae—come over here and feel these hard tomatoes.

ACTOR 2: *(Move tomato and speaks)* Put that down or buy it Miss.

ACTOR 5: *(Squeezing tomatoes with zest)* I love these, they're the biggest I've ever seen. Ella Mae—!!

ACTOR 2: Oh, Ella Mae, will pay. Hey, Ella Mae—prime tomatoes.

ACTOR 3: *(Taking ACTOR 5 by arm)* Come darling, we're not buying vegetables today *(She makes a sweeping gesture and exits).*

ACTOR 5: *(As she squeezes a few more, she says to audience)* Don't you love tomatoes that big. Don't you love tomatoes that red!

(Looks around and grabs a tomato—she sneaks off pulling it and the actor connected to it with her).

(The disgusted vendor [ACTOR 2] exits after them.)

(Blackout)

(Slides of food: health food, grocery store displays, cans, produce, outdoor displays, candy, meat…)

(A giant, one-dimensional hand, two ACTORS behind to operate it, moves center stage, holds, then backs off. HE and SHE are shoved in from right and left stage by two giant plastic hands. It takes several pushes to get HE and SHE center. They are nose to nose but the hands are right behind them to make sure they stay close for this scene. HE reads from teleprompter left.)

HE: I'm glad the Republicans got into office, it will sober up ths whole country. That generation has been

wanting to get even with us for at least twelve years.
It'll be interesting to see how they choose to go about
it. Do you think they'll cut off food stamps first or the
public works projects...?

(Giant hand smacks HE's hand.)

SHE: Don't talk like that

(Giant hand covers HE's mouth.)

HE: I'm not talking politics, I'm just pointing out
possible drastic changes in the lifestyles of many of our
friends. *(HE removes hand from mouth.)* Luckily you and
I have never depended upon outside forces...

(Hands shove HE and SHE tightly together).

SHE: There's something wrong in the way you....

HE: You don't have to agree with the thoughts I'm
trying to convey, but I do expect...

(Giant hand gestures to SHE's ear.)

SHE: I wasn't listening to your thoughts.

(Hand hits HE).

HE: I don't get it, I usually know what you're going to
say before you say it.

SHE: It's the tone.

HE: Tone?

(Hand quivers and backs slightly.)

SHE: You're sounding too nice, too like an actor, too
like a President.

HE: God forbid.

SHE: You must be thinking again.

(Hand pats HE's shoulder.)

SHE: T-V brainwash!

HE: I wasn't aware—

(SHE's *plastic hand points with strong gestures in several directions.*)

SHE: I want that old edge in your voice, the impersonal menace, the hollow cheek bone, the slight curl at the edge of your lip…the hardedged whine.

(*Hand wags finger three times at he. Hands grab* HE *and* SHE *and pull them off left and right.*)

(*Percussion, slow steady beat on casaba [rattle]. actors enter, march in rhythm—form a semicircle. an actor initiates a simple physical movement, e g hands together at chest and open to side. This repeats in rhythms. as rhythm intensifies, the physical movements of the actors should give one the feeling of "video space invaders" moving closer and closer.* ACTOR *who is to play the "feelings" scene comes to center of playing area and tries to project as many feelings as possible. One of the actors bumps maliciously into her to help her feel, others continue the rhythm which gradually increases in speed and intensity. One at a time the actors in the semicircle come forward and do something to the center actor to make her feel, e. g. scratching her face while pulling her hair, slow motion shoving, belly bounces, tapping on her shoulders, rubbing up and down body, a hug, little kisses all over…*)

(HE *and* SHE *dress during this.* HE *in smoking jacket,* SHE *in long negligee with feathers.*)

ACTOR 4: I love feelings…even depressions. It's reassuring to feel adrenalin coursing through my body even if it's triggered by anger at the potholes on Martha Street as they break another hole in my Midas muffler. (ACTOR *scratches her face off*). They say adrenalin can increase your blood pressure, but the reassurance of having real feelings cancels out that negative for me. (ACTOR *tries with force to shove her over*). Some people I know would rather think, would rather bet their life on their IQ, but I believe in the integrity of my feelings

(Several ACTORS *poke at her to get her attention).*

ACTOR 4: I absolutely adore anyone who helps me exercise my feelings; even if I hate that person— because at the same time I'm feeling hate, I have to admit I totally enjoy the fact that I can feel that feeling—HATRED—HATRED—HAT—RED RED HAT HATE. I have the right to feel that feeling *(*ACTOR *rubs.)* The feeling inside of me that I cultivate most of all though—is yearning— *(*ACTOR *alternates hugging and protection gestures.)*

I love to be in love so I can yearn and pine for the object of my love. *(Hugs begin here)* I spend days picking out tunes that have that yearning sound...

(Piaf, etc. Collect some yearning music from the group).

*(*ACTOR *tries to get her attention. She doesn't notice.)*

ACTOR 4: I set aside one hour each day to exercise my feelings through yearning music, even if I don't have a live object near by. I shuffle my eyepod...

*(*ACTOR *slaps her and exits, other actors gather around and tickle or massage her foot and/or shoulders, etc. This builds)*

ACTOR 4: ...then I lie on my stomach on top of a sheepskin, so air will circulate under by body. I listen and yearn, and listen and yearn until the tears flow. I cry and cry and smell the smell of the sheepskin. I don't have as much time for this luxury as I would like because the main problem is

(All ACTORS *turn their backs on her and exit)*

ACTOR 4: I don't fall in love that often.

*(*HE *and* SHE *pose,* SHE *right,* HE *left, on each side of platform.)*

(ACTORS *enter, dancing with manikin parts. They slow
dance as if the single arm, or hand, or leg they dance with
is the whole lover. A medley of love songs is sung by* HE
and SHE *as they dance.* SHE *is accompanied on piano, he
on guitar. [no more than one or two bars of each song.]
"Feelings" is played first as an instrumental.*)

SHE: "Cry me a river, cry me a river, I cried a river
over…"

HE: "I've been thinking now for a long, long time how
to go my own separate way."

SHE: "It was just one of those nights, just one of those
fabulous flights, a trip to the moon."

HE: "There's a lady who's sure all that glitters is gold,
she's buying the stairway to heaven."

SHE: "You're a sweetheart if there ever was one."

(Till We Meet Again *as an instrumental*)

(ACTORS *continue dancing with manikin parts.*)

(HE *and* SHE *begin to relate to a manikin part.* SHE *cuddles
with a bust,* HE *strokes the head of an armless figure
positioned at his side of the platform. They smoke "play"
cigarettes—the kind that puff talcum power—and objectively
relate to their love objects.* SHE *lounges on right side of
platform.* HE *stands left.* SHE *reads from left teleprompter,
he reads from right. Romantic music plays throughout.*)

SHE: Did you enjoy last night?

HE: I prefer today.

SHE: Just answer me one question.

HE: I'm already ahead.

SHE: You didn't?

HE: After awhile.

SHE: But did you experience enjoyment?

HE: Teasing's okay, up to a point.

SHE: I didn't think of it as teasing.

HE: All right, the edge of torture can be stimulating, for a change.

SHE: *(Smiles)* Torture was the furthest from my images.

HE: What did you think you were doing?

SHE: As you so often request, I wasn't thinking.

HE: Good.

SHE: Just showing you what I like.

HE: What was it?

(HE and SHE dance with their "parts". At a random moment, they put the manikin parts down and change costumes. All continue dancing. The following lines come out of the manikin part dance. HE and SHE leave their platform and arrange each actor with a manikin part. The object is to create an objective relationship, e. g. he places a manikin hand over an actor's face. SHE places manikin legs around an actor's neck. SHE might place this actor on the floor, legs up and place the manikin legs up too. They continue this throughout the scene.)

(ACTORS take lines to their manikin part.)

ACTOR 3: What I like about myself is my breathy voice.

ACTOR 1: Yes, I agree, I'm bored with these assertive voices. Firmess is so aggressive.

ACTOR 2: What I like about myself is my mediumness, not too thin and no thick tires.

ACTOR 5: I like the way I come down stairs, just right.

ACTOR 1: It's true, I hate those people who clump.

ACTOR 4: I like the way I drive a car. I know what I'm doing. I'm one with the engine, I thrust with the hood.

ACTOR 5: I like sitting beside you when you do that.

ACTOR 3: I really love my ability to buy meat. Did I tell you how my grandfather taught me to buy meat? I know just how to look for the marbling in the meat. Every piece I buy is tender or I take it back.

ACTOR 5: I love the way your— *(Sweater, blouse, shirt, etc.)* —hangs on you. It flows with your body as you walk.

ACTOR 4: I love the way you walk, I get off on the bounce of your hips.

ACTOR 5: I didn't know you looked at me when I wasn't looking at you.

ACTOR 4: One of my several pleasures.

ACTOR 1: I'm mad about the cut of your nose. It's fascinating how a centimeter of cartilage this way or that, determines whether we fall madly in love or not.

ACTOR 2: And have you fallen madly?

ACTOR 1: Each time I embrace your nose.

(Music begins— "one way love".)

(ACTORS remain totally uninvolved in the emotions of the song: they are detached, tough, objective. as they sing, they perform aggressive, abstract, physical isolations.)

(The song begins with isolations performed during the instrumental introduction. [x] indicates isolation changes.)

One Way Love

(X) Making love is a cup of tea, to me,
Sex is chewing gum.
Kissing takes the place of
Brushing your teeth,
(X) Don't you see—
(X) Romantic love is dumb!
(X) Romantic love is dumb!
(Isolations [X]. Constant movement, repeated jumps, in and

out with elbows.)
Only dopes, only dips, Pisces and
(X) Taurus trips still believe in love.
(X) I'm above it all,
(X) I won't ever fall,
Because
(X) Love is best when it's numb!
(X) Love is best when it's numb!
(X) Love is best when it's numb!
(Isolations) (X).
(X) Romantic love is dumb,
(X) Romantic love is dumb,
(X) Sex is best when I'm numb;
Gonna go get me some!
(X) Sex is best when I'm numb,
Gonna go get me some!
(X) Sex is best when I'm numb;
Sex is best when I'm numb;
Gonna go get me some!
Gonna go get me some!
(As the actors exit, repeat phrases of last line)
Gonna go… Sex… Gonna… Get… Some… Go-Go…
Get some…

(Alone on right side of platform HE *plays with* SHE's *toes and rocks back and forth. he reads from teleprompter right.)*

*(*ACTORS's *heads appear from behind downstage cubes. their faces are blank—relaxed; each expresses an attitude or a desire, which makes a facial mask appear slowly on each face. The expression arrives, takes over, is established, then vanishes.)*

HE: *(Alone)* I'm not used to it. I examine myself and find my heart bursts with happiness. This is discouraging because I'd rather stay cool and on an even keel. Happiness is disturbing—it implies a crash is just around the corner. *(Notices a warmth)* The sun's out. We've had more sunlight than usual. That could be it. In the past, I've noticed an inner smile within myself whenever there's been lots of sunlight. *(Muses over this)*

(Two ACTORS *working on objective expressions sit on the cubes. Two other* ACTORS *wearing long white gloves are hidden behind* ACTORS 1 *and 3 and the cube. The four white-gloved hands appear from the sides of* ACTORS 1 *and 3 and carefully arrange* ACTORS's *hair as they speak.* ACTORS 1 *and 3 speak as if they can constantly see an image of themselves. They are on a bus, side by side; they speak as long time friends.)*

ACTOR 3: I don't like to wear my hair bobbed.

ACTOR 1: I like to keep my hair this length.

ACTOR 3: You can—your hair has more body than mine.

ACTOR 1: Mine's thick.

ACTOR 3: Yours has more body—mine's so soft. If I had it short I'd have to curl it every night.

ACTOR 1: A permanent?

ACTOR 3: Oh, I don't like perms.

ACTOR 1: I don't like perms.

ACTOR 3: No, I'd have to put it in rollers—but my hair's just so soft, the rollers help to give it body. You can see—my hair isn't curly. Your hair will hold a curl—your hair has lots of body.

ACTOR 1: My whole family has strong hair.

(On the upper platform, SHE *puts on a white plastic bib.* SHE *assumes a cheesecake pose, face front, butt to side. Two* ACTORS *enter, each wears a giant cellophane bag. One* ACTOR *has some bright blue facial mask cream which the* ACTOR *carefully applies all over* SHE's *face. The other* ACTOR *in cellophane has a hair dryer which is held on* SHE's

face to speed the drying process. SHE *speaks through this entire process, reading from the teleprompter left.)*

SHE: I'm putting all my faith in my new strawberry facial mask. I have a genetic inheritance toward frown lines on my forehead. He thinks I'm thinking when he sees those lines deepen, but most of the time I'm just trying to see him better. Talking doesn't convince. If this strawberry facial mask doesn't suppress my pseudo-thinking lines, I'll try that plastic cosmetic spray the television starlets wear. In the meantime, Scotch strapping tape might do, but I mustn't pull my skin. He gets so annoyed. My skin could become our battle ground—I must make it a neutral area.

(The two ACTORSs *complete the facial and exit. A black hooded* ACTOR *enters, runs center and says, "i object", then runs off.)*

(Blackout)

(Slides of beautiful animals and children appear.)

*(*ACTOR 3 *[as a mother] and* ACTORS 2 *and* 4 *[as children] sit on the down left cube.* ACTOR 1 *[as grandmother] stands on down right cube. actors playing children pick up manikin parts and dice and play. They exclaim, "eye object", when they find delight in their objects. Mother watches over her children. Grandmother incants over the soft-sculpture dice she holds.)*

ACTOR 3: Numbers are beautiful because they are pure and perfect symbols that say exactly what they mean. Numbers are what they are and don't fool you like the changing masks of a movie star...or a false lover.

ACTOR 2: What's ten?

ACTOR 4: Angelina Jolie!

ACTOR 2: If a number is pure, how can a woman be ten?

ACTOR 4: She's thirty-six, twenty-six, thirty-six.

ACTOR 3: Those are double numbers, double crossed and therefore, impure.

ACTOR 2: What's four?

ACTOR 3: As many as we are here. One-two-three-four. There we are—we're four—no less-no more.

ACTOR 1: *(Incants)* Four you can see with your outside eyes but there are generations residing within me— some are more to the fore from time to time than others. For instance, my patriotic Daddy wants into this discussion— *(Looks over her shoulder)* He says we must not forget— *(Becomes Father)* "There were those before and heretofore, and moreover our dear foremothers and forefathers who loved us fourfold. This was recorded by the fourth estate, including some foreigners who weren't so forthcoming as they might have been. Furthermore, the forceful Fourth Division hurled four hundred tanks into the Black Forest, then fell back four kilometers for rest and relaxation before hurling themselves again at the four corners of the world. Henceforth, I vowed to keep my four eyes peeled on all enemy forces forever."

ACTOR 4: One to nine and back again?

ACTOR 1: *(Incants)* The devil's number is 666.

ACTOR 2: That adds up to nine.

ACTOR 1: *(Incants to dice)* Nine's trouble—double trouble. *(To audience)* God's system is binary, one plus zero.

ACTOR 3: *(Correcting Grandma)* That's not God's, *(Stands, smiling)* that's I B M's! *(Teaching her children)* The pure language of the computer is the combination of zero plus one, one plus zero in combination into the infinite. With those two symbols all problems are solved.

ACTOR 1: All problems?

ACTOR 3: To do with math. The world of purest beauty is in the world of numbers. The universe gives up her secrets when the correct equation is formed.

ACTOR 2: It's too far to see.

ACTOR 1: No it isn't.

ACTOR 3: It's all in here— *(Tapping child's head)* That's why it's beautiful.

ACTOR 4: The inside of his head isn't beautiful, it's full of…

ACTOR 1: Numbers.

ACTOR 3: *(Sings to Grandma)* "I've got your number."

ACTOR 1: *(To mother)* You're my number one.

ACTOR 3: *(To her children)* You're first in my heart.

ACTOR 2: *(Starts to get up)* Last one in's a rotten number.

ACTOR 1: There are no rotten numbers.

ACTOR 3: Only wrong thinking about numbers. You can say anything with numbers.

ACTOR 4: I want to go number two.

(Blackout)

(ACTOR 5 enters wearing black hood, comes center and says, "i object". ACTORS 2, 3, 4 on stage left cube, put on black hoods and in unison say, "i object." They exit.)

(SHE enters. SHE wears a revealing dance outfit with matching hat and bag. SHE stands on cube down left.)

(ACTORS 2, 3, and 4 are SHE's friends. They pace and lament—trying to be objective. They often stop, pose and contemplate their plight.)

(SHE's lines in this scene are memorized.)

ACTOR 4: I don't like the way things are going.

SHE: You're feeling again?

ACTOR 2: Feeling bad.

SHE: Stop thinking about your feelings.

ACTOR 3: He makes me feel this say.

SHE: Only if you want to.

ACTOR 4: I haven't slept all night.

SHE: Did he sleep?

ACTOR 2: Out like a light.

SHE: You stayed up?

ACTOR 3: We had a terrible fight.

SHE: That was a mistake.

ACTOR 4: He started it.

SHE: Let him fight alone.

ACTOR 2: That's easy for you to say, you don't have to live with him.

SHE: I don't have to live with anyone.

ACTOR 3: You live with him.

SHE: I chose to.

ACTOR 4: Well, he must make you feel good.

SHE: I'm not into feeling.

(The friends are startled—they double take out front, then exit. SHE stays, posing on cube during the following.)

(The following image is about objective meeting—
1. ACTORS 1 and 2 cross the stage waving. 1 thinks 2 is waving to him, but she is waving to someone else.
2. ACTORS 3 and 4 run to embrace one another. ACTOR 3 was looking to embrace a child and so ducks and the hug is not exchanged.)

(Three or four other miscalculated meetings should be performed. the last two ACTORS *meet center, turn to the audience and say:)*

ACTOR 4: Hi, I'm only ten and I'm four-feet, eleven inches.

ACTOR 5: Hi, I'm only eighty-four and I'm four-feet, ten inches.

HE: *(On right side of platform)* What images do you have when we make love?

SHE: *(On left cube)* The fingers of Saturn's rings.

(HE *jumps down, crosses to* SHE *and slowly peels off the, now dried, facial mask.)*

(Blackout)

(Slides of flowers and animals appear.)

(During black, ACTOR 2 *gets into position center stage with either a real, or small toy motorcycle.)*

ACTOR 2: *(Crawling out from under bike)* It's relaxing to work on my bike. Bikes are so contained, you can lose yourself taking them apart. I love to polish my engine. The machine—it's aesthetically pleasing—in itself. Same reason that I like a ten-speed—you have to balance it. *(Stands)* I thought I was different from those guys who like bikes for a power trip, those guys who like a bike to extend, y'know, their phallic symbol… People that really care about their bikes show it, not so much by the way they drive it, but by the way they take care of it— *(Begins to caress bike)* Polish the fenders, tune the engine, oil the clutch assembly— *(Does this)* —one down, three up. I don't think it has to be a power trip. There's nothing like grabbing ahold of the handle bars— *(Does this)* and easing your body over the seat, then ya sit down on that real leather cushion of a Harley Six Hundred. *(Really gets into it— the fantasy builds.)* Check the clutch. *(Turns on ignition)*

RRRMMMMMMMMMMMMmmmmmmmmmmmm
ahahahahahahahahaha. Oh it's a perfect tool! Yeah,
there's nothing like going down the street on one
of these. Rrrrmmmmmmm. At first I was cautious,
considerate of pedestrians, tried not to make a whole
lot of noise. But then, especially if the weather was
nice and the machine was working well, I found
myself revving the machine higher, and going faster
and faster until I got out into the open country and
then I'd let it go as fast as I possibly could, and I'd
take off and pull the front wheel up into the air,
let it down, then rev the engine RRRmmmmmm,
check it out, and… Get out the way you stupid
idiot!… Engine's perfect. RRRmmmm… I hate dogs!
RRRRRR MMMMMMMMMhahahahaha I love
my motorcycle! RRRRRMMMMMMMMMMMMM
I love the feeling of being on one of these things!
Rmmmmmmmmm, I went as fast as I possibly could,
then I got careless and didn't watch where I was going.
I started looking behind me, and there I am, going
right toward a tree! (ACTOR *and the bike topple over.*) The
last thing I remember is covering my face like this…
(Picks up the bike and offers it) "Anybody wanna buy a
used bike?"

(Blackout)

(More slides)

*(*HE *and* SHE *lounge against one another on right side of
platform. Both speeches are on both prompters.* HE *and* SHE
*read first from one, then from the other. They wear dressing
gowns—*SHE, *a short, white embroidered satin kimona,* HE,
a long, rich blue. ACTOR 5 *fans them with palm leaves as
they are being fed brie and sliced apples by* ACTORS 1 *and* 4
who wear tuxes and carry linen towels over their arms. HE
and SHE *are stoned.)*

HE: If I can be up to the minute—or just ahead of the trend—if I can see the images coming before they get here, then time won't be going by because I'll always be going to meet it.

SHE: I've got to take the time to find out about making a will. I'd hate to find myself dead in a car crash with my eyes useless. My eyes have the possibility of going on living forever into the future. Maybe I can write the will in such a way that whoever inherits my eyes, will in turn have to will them to an organ bank, and then they'll be implanted in someone else who needs eyes, and someone else and someone else and someone else. I'm going to do it. This way I'll get to see forever. *(She is pleased.)*

(They continue eating and dreaming for several beats.)

(During the following scene SHE *takes off kimona and paces the floor.* SHE *is anxious for* HE *to arrive.* HE *enters in black leather jacket.)*

(Other ACTORS *come from stage right and left, meet at center, and say to the audience:)*

ACTOR 2: Hi, I bought my house only five years ago and now it's worth twice as much as I paid for it.

ACTOR 3: Hi, I bought my house forty years ago and now the dollar is worth twenty-four cents.

*(*HE *paces too and gives* SHE *orders.)*

HE: Put on that old dress I bought you.

SHE: Which one?

HE: The one from the Pike Street Market in Seattle.

SHE: Are you sure you want me to wear that one?

HE: Yes.

SHE: Wouldn't you rather look at the one from Garbo's Closet?

HE: I know it too well.

SHE: Did you get me two dresses in Seattle?

HE: A dress and a jacket.

SHE: I thought it was two dresses.

HE: You can't remember anything.

SHE: I remember you.

HE: Put it on.

SHE: Now?

HE: I'm lonesome.

SHE: *(Poses)* I'm here.

HE: (HE *gazes off and remembers.* HE *poses.* SHE *finds the dress.)* I'm lonesome for Seattle, for the dress hanging on that rack at the open market overlooking Puget Sound. It was framed by two ocean-going freighters. We waited to buy it after a sudden rain followed by a rainbow.

SHE: *(Holding it up)* Dress? *(She dances with it. She puts it on.)*

HE: *(He sighs but doesn't look—his imagination is better than the real thing)* Yes, yes. I love you in that dress. Put it on. I can't wait, I love you in that dress. Put it on. It was made for you.

SHE: Zip me?

HE: *(Hesitates then zips the dress. Feels dress)* Oh, I love the feel of it. They don't make material like this anymore. Stand back. Walk away from me. Walk to the right, walk to the left. It was made for you.

SHE: Are the shoulders correct?

HE: *(He lies on floor)* Perfect. Walk toward me.

(SHE *walks right over* HE.)

HE: Ahhhhhhh. Made for you. Made for you. I love you in this dress.

(All ACTORS *enter with objects they love—their personal favorite objects. They relate to these during the following scene.)*

*(*HE *and* SHE *face each other. Each is the other's love object. They relate.)*

(The following lines are overlapped. but, time may be taken within some lines.)

SHE: *(They tango)* You're as macho as split ends.

HE: *(Tango front. They turn to back wall)* You're as sweet as spiked heels.

SHE: You're as strong as saliva.

HE: *(Tango front. They turn to back wall)* You're as weak as ocean waves.

ACTOR 5: You're as attractive as Tequila.

ACTOR 2: You're as handsome as gas and oil.

ACTOR 4: You're as beautiful as soybeans.

ACTOR 1: I respect you like cancer.

ACTOR 3: I want you like water.

ACTOR 4: Your ears are textbooks.

ACTOR 2: You look like withdrawal symptoms.

HE: You come like a fire engine.

SHE: You come like a marigold.

ACTOR 3: Your teeth are a can opener.

ACTOR 4: Your muscles are tire irons.

ACTOR 2: Your tongue is calves liver.

ACTOR 1: Your touch is a dirt bike.

ACTOR 4: Your nails are Coke bottle caps.

SHE: Your mind's as fast as wrinkles.

HE: Your ass is Missouri marble.

ACTOR 3: You talk like a robot car painter.

ACTOR 4: You kiss like the Half-Price Store.

ACTOR 2: You smell like cement.

ACTOR 1: Your hair is astro turf after a mud slide.

ACTOR 2: Your presence is crazy glue.

ACTOR 5: Your eyes are methedrine.

ACTOR 3: You're as smart as Mount Rushmore.

ACTOR 2: Your blood is full of sharks.

ACTOR 5: Your mind is the Yellow Pages.

SHE: Loving you is a hangover.

HE: Your will is cockroach eggs.

ACTOR 4: Your laugh is the grave.

ACTOR 2: Your nipples are vampire fangs.

ACTOR 5: You're as funny as linoleum.

ACTOR 1: Your brain has lost weight.

ACTOR 3: Your skin is Hanscom Park.

ACTOR 5: Your hugs are hamburger.

ACTOR 4: You're as faithful as inter-stellar space dust.

ACTOR 2: You're as solid as moonlight.

ACTOR 1: You're as fast as rush hour traffic.

SHE: Your love making is a nest of cobras.

ACTOR 4: Your hips are a hydraulic jack.

ACTOR 3: Your tongue is a snail darter.

ACTOR 2: Your belly feels like aluminum foil.

ACTOR 1: You're as exciting as Sunday morning television.

HE: Your breath is air conditioned.

(*All* ACTORS *suddenly sing*)

Occupied Territory
(Song)

This is occupied territory
We live in occupied territory.
Are you ready to live
Beyond your fingernail?
There is a vast body to behold—
That body is you. I implore you to swim into the
Mainstream of your own conscious being,
And live in your whole body, too.
Aren't you cramped there under that
Damp, dirty nail? Expand outward into your fist, and
Let your mind exist in
Your chest and rise upward to
The tip of your breast.
Ahhhhhhhh yes she feels so good—
And you can feel you if you only would.
This is a tiny game,
But it can extend when you are far from me.
Let me hold your hand
And you can live here safely in my land.
I won't give anyone your
Phone number.
But you can call me any time—
Night or day—
And we will—Fling our arms around each other—
And lay and lay and lay
And lay and lay
And lay.

(*Scene resumes as before.*)

ACTOR 2: Your fingers are potato peelers.

ACTOR 3: You sing like airplanes.

ACTOR 5: You're armpits are the Henry Doorly Zoo.

ACTOR 1: Your hands are cowboy boots.

ACTOR 2: Your love making is butter and garlic spaghetti.

ACTOR 4: Your word is armed robbery.

ACTOR 2: Your eyes are grease pits.

ACTOR 3: Your face is a Norman Rockwell Christmas Plate.

ACTOR 5: You cook like Seventy-Second Street.

ACTOR 3: You taste like Comet cleanser.

ACTOR 2: Your mouth is a police car.

ACTOR 1: Your arms are roller coasters.

ACTOR 4: Your toes are whips.

ACTOR 3: Your legs are Carter Lake.

SHE: Your guts are the stock yards.

HE: You're full of Falstaff. *(A local beer)*

ACTOR 3: You're as reliable as the dollar.

ACTOR 2: Your cock is hair spray.

ACTOR 1: Your breasts are thumb tacks.

ACTOR 5: Your love is French fried.

ACTOR 2: Your love is Purina Cat Chow.

HE & SHE: Our love is a frisbee.

(HE and SHE each throw a frisbee into the audience. Smiling, the entire company throws frisbees to the audience.)

(Music up)

END OF PLAY